A DAY IN THE LIFE OF AN
Illustrator

by Ken Witty

Photography by Stephen Sanacore

Troll Associates

Library of Congress Catalog Card Number: 80-54100
ISBN 0-89375-448-X   ISBN 0-89375-449-8   Paper Edition

Sally Vitsky is a free-lance illustrator. Free-lancers work for themselves, and must sell their artwork to earn a living. Sally's office is in her apartment. There, she begins her workday by calling clients to whom she hopes to sell her illustrations.

After her morning telephone calls, Sally packs up
her portfolio. The illustrations in her portfolio rep-
resent some of Sally's best work. She continually
changes them and adds new ones, so she can show
clients the full range of her talents. Getting new
work depends on the quality of Sally's portfolio.

Now she is off to a series of appointments. Sally has lived in this city since she came here to go to school. She enjoys the excitement of the city and the free-lancer's way of life—never knowing what the new day may bring. Perhaps today Sally will get an exciting new assignment.

Portfolio "dropoff" is a necessary part of any free-lance illustrator's job. Once a week, illustrators leave samples of their work at television studios, magazine publishers, and other places that need artwork. A receptionist at a television station makes out a receipt for Sally's portfolio. Sally will return for her portfolio later.

Next, she keeps an appointment with a new client—a national news agency. The news agency sends slides or photographs to television stations that don't have their own art departments. Sally must have a special piece of art ready by the next morning. Her new client shows her some examples of what is needed.

Her next appointment is with a client who provides decorative pieces for store windows and restaurants. He hires artists like Sally to come up with fanciful creations. She shows him a sketch of one of her new designs.

Like other illustrators, Sally has her own personal style. Colorful paper cutouts are her specialty. After the sketch of a design is approved by a client, Sally develops it into a three-dimensional paper cutout. These colorful cutouts were used as part of a window display in a jewelry store.

Sally meets a fellow illustrator at a midtown restaurant for lunch. Since free-lancers work alone, they welcome the opportunity to see friends and exchange the latest news at lunch. Sally and her friend both went to the same art school.

After lunch, they stop in to see a graphic arts exhi-
bition. Here the country's top illustrators show
their work. Sally tries to keep up with what is
happening in the art world. She hopes someday to
have her work included in shows like this one.

Before going home to begin her afternoon work, Sally visits an art store to stock up on supplies. Her cutouts require colored paper, glue, spray varnish, paint, and balsa wood. If she runs out of any of these materials, she may be unable to finish an assignment on time.

The salesperson shows Sally a new airbrush. An airbrush is an artists' tool that sprays paint in a very fine mist. It is used to shade or tint small areas. Sally wants to replace the old airbrush she has at home, but she will look in several stores before deciding which model to buy.

Back at home Sally gets down to work. She uses a drafting table instead of a desk. Nearby shelves are stocked with supplies, and wide drawers hold artwork. Sally is completing a cutout that will appear in a magazine.

Sally has worked on this figure for many days. First came the sketch of the design. With a pencil and pad, Sally drew the general idea of what she wanted to create. That is the hardest part—thinking up clever ideas. Sally often makes many sketches before she is satisfied.

Sally's cutouts are built up piece by piece. The basic figure is already finished. Now she is making the final addition—the words spoken by the figure in her cutout. She makes a pattern for the letters on white paper, then uses the pattern to cut the final letters from colored paper.

Next Sally uses her airbrush to shade portions of the letters. This makes them look less flat. Then she glues a small piece of balsa wood on the back of each letter so there will be some space between them when they are glued together. When she assembles the letters, the shading and spacing add life to the words.

With the addition of the final lettering, Sally's cut-out illustration is finished. The next step is to take it to a photographer's studio to have it photographed. The resulting slide will be sent to the magazine.

Several other photographs of Sally's work have just
been completed. She and the photographer examine
them on a light box. They must be sure the trans-
parencies are neither too light nor too dark. These
are fine, and can be sent to the client.

Sally picks up her portfolio at the television station. This dropoff did not result in a new assignment. Being a free-lancer is fun, but it can also be difficult. There are no regular paychecks, and there may be long stretches without work.

One of the business firms that Sally deals with frequently is a photostat house. This is where artwork and lettering are enlarged or reduced in size. Sally gives exact instructions for the size of the photostats she needs for a particular job.

Like other illustrators, Sally must continually think up new ways to attract clients. One of the ways she finds new business is by sending out postcards that show her work. She has them made at a printing shop. These latest samples came out very well.

Another frequent stop is the post office, where Sally addresses and mails her postcards. She sends out a dozen or more every week to possible clients. Then she follows up her mailings with telephone calls and personal appointments.

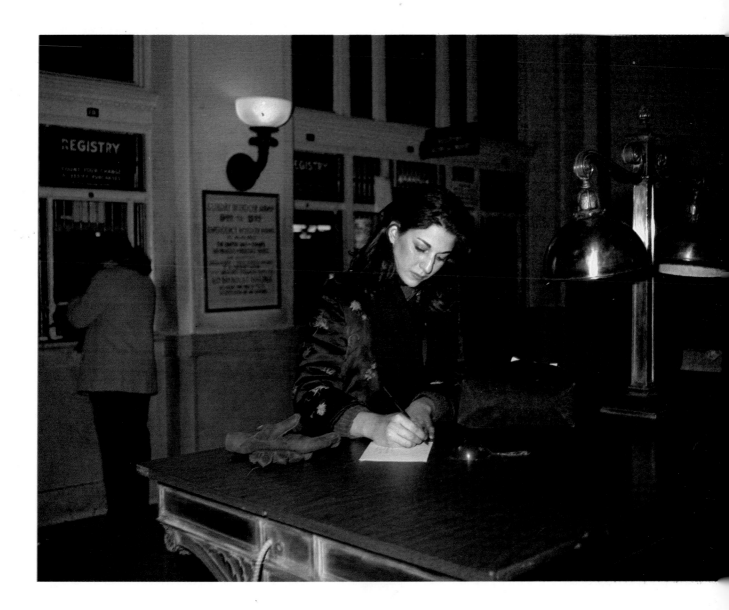

Free-lancers spend a lot of time looking for new assignments. At a meeting with the art director of a magazine, Sally shows some examples of work she has done for similar magazines. The art director is impressed with Sally's work, and says she would like to use her in the future.

Pleased with this success, Sally rewards herself with a visit to an antique store. She likes to collect antiques, particularly glassware, like this pitcher. She has had her eye on this piece for some time. The price is within reach, so she buys it.

Sally's interest in antiques serves a double purpose. First, there is the enjoyment of being a collector. But there is also a professional reason. Sally uses her purchases as subjects for her sketches and as inspiration for new ideas.

She keeps her skills sharpened by attending art class once a week. The class is held in a famous art club, where artists have gathered for more than a century. Here Sally can practice the skills she has, and learn new ones.

After class, Sally returns home for a late dinner with her sister, Pat. Pat brought a special kind of cheese pie. Sally made a salad. Sally and her sister seldom have time to prepare complicated meals. They often share the cooking this way.

At eleven o'clock, they watch the news and weather.
Sally tries to catch as many news broadcasts as she
can. This frequently helps her in her work. She also
studies the artwork that is used by the various TV
stations, and compares it to her own work.

Sally's work for the news agency is still ahead of her. The assignment discussed this morning is a piece of art to be used with a news story on rising taxes. She uses special "transfer type" to print the letters of the word TAXES on a bright background.

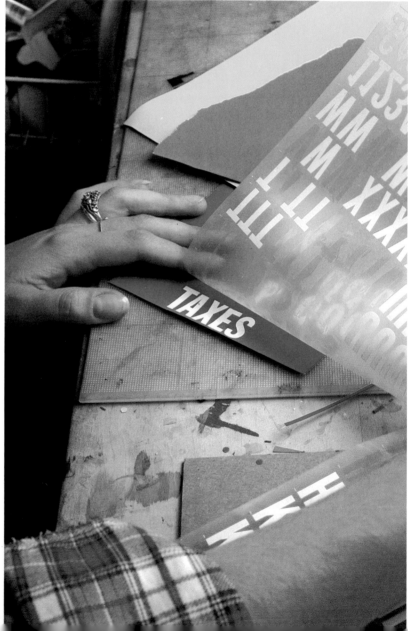

Then she adds a brightly colored arrow, to show where taxes are heading. Slides for news stories must often be ready for the next day's broadcasts. That means Sally often finds herself working past midnight to complete assignments like this.

Late at night is the time Sally often gets her best ideas. A new design for the restaurant display has occurred to her. She will sketch it out before she goes to bed. Sally is tired from her long day, but she never tires of her work as an illustrator.